WINTER WINGS

BIRDS OF THE NORTHERN ROCKIES

BY BERT RAYNES

PHOTOGRAPHY BY
THOMAS D. MANGELSEN

Photographs © 2003 Thomas D. Mangelsen

Text © 2003 Bert Raynes

Design by Beth Frye, John McGauvran

Production coordination by Janet Goodman

Printed in the United States of America through Moore-Wallace

First Printing 2003

Photo credits:

Jack Dykinga - Thomas D. Mangelsen biography photo

Lucas J. Gilman of The Jackson Hole News and Guide - Bert Raynes biography photo

Library of Congress Publisher's Cataloging–in–Publication Data

Raynes, Bert.
    Winter wings/by Bert Raynes ; photography by Thomas
D. Mangelsen
    p. cm.
    Includes index.
    ISBN 1-890310-35-2
    1. Birds––Rocky Mountains.   I. Mangelsen, Thomas D.
II. Title.
QL683.R63R39 2003   598'.0978
                         QBI03-200434

Provided in cooperation with Quality Books, Inc.

To the wild things whose courage and wit help
them survive winters in Northern climes.

~ Bert Raynes

To Spencer Wilson, "Pops," best friend and mentor. Spence
exemplifies the goodness and potential of the human spirit. From
helping underprivileged children in California to protecting
cougars in Colorado and Wyoming, at the young age of 91, "Pops"
continues his mission to make the world a better place. Thanks
for the voyage, for enriching my days, for making me laugh, and
for opening my eyes wide to life and even to the birds of winter.

~ Tom Mangelsen

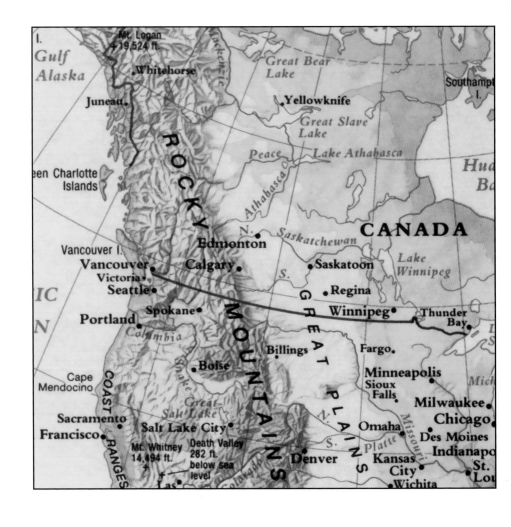

✌ TABLE OF CONTENTS ✍

FOREWORD ☞

Winters in Northern Rocky Mountain states can be impressive with their extremes of cold, snow and vastness. An apparent lack of winter bird activity can accentuate the inhospitable feelings challenging a visitor or newcomer from milder climates. A trip through *Winter Wings* paints a different picture and warms one's consciousness of wintering avifauna as the reader learns about the more common species of birds.

The author, Bert Raynes, has written a book that is simply a pleasure to read. I started reading *Winter Wings* with the intent of providing comments to the author. I found that as soon as I finished reading about one species, I was eagerly awaiting the presentation of the next species. I quickly forgot about my "task-orientated attack" and finished reading the manuscript without one written comment.

What Bert has done is to combine the interesting elements of natural history and behavior with the most important aspects of identification and habitat use associated with each species. There is no attempt to "dump" all of Bert's knowledge about each species onto the reader. A lot of us learn and remember easiest by associating dry facts with interesting pieces of information. Carefully selected facts most important for identification, knowing where to find birds and understanding how they make a living are presented with a memory-enhancing narrative and photographs.

Winter Wings is generously embellished with photographs by Tom Mangelsen. Most wildlife enthusiasts are familiar with Tom's talent and the many inspiring scenes captured on film that are available through his company, Images of Nature®. However, I cannot help but point out that some of his most sought-after and heart-warming photos in recent years are of wildlife in the most arctic settings imaginable. How fitting it is for a book on winter birds to contain a collection of Mangelsen's photographs. Even if Tom's task were to provide photographs that illustrate and assist identification of species, I believe the photographs will be of special interest and favorites for many owners of the book.

Bird enthusiasts who read this book likely will find that they have retained a wealth of information that will accompany them and their field guides on their next winter outing to observe birds. Advanced birders will find the book refreshing their enthusiasm for birds.

Bob Oakleaf
Non-Game Biologist
Wyoming Game & Fish Department

PERSONAL, BY THE SCRIBBLER ✍

I am grateful for many reasons. First and foremost of all, for my beloved wife, Meg Raynes, without whom I would have never accomplished a thing.

More specifically, those who really helped me concoct this volume include: a legion of writers whose words influence me each time I read them, words I have consciously attempted not to copy despite my continuing admiration and perusal of them; companionable bird watchers; botanists; geologists; insect-oriented types; photographers; students of history and hikers by the score who were and are almost invariably helpful, sharing and instructive; Jackson Hole Bird Club members; faithful readers of the "Far Afield" column in the Jackson Hole (Wyoming) News and Guide; friends.

Even more precisely, with respect to this volume, my gratitude goes to Mary Gerty, who accepted the task of interpreting my handwriting with grace and even with anticipation and eagerness; Karla Swiggum; Karilyn Brodell; Dan Fulton; Ruth Shea; Rod Drewein; Victoria Blumberg; Louise Lasley; Chris Mather; Kacy Painter; Jan Hayse; Mike Casey; Walter Mather; Cara Blessley Lowe; Krissy Robertson; Jim Stanford; John McGauvran; Beth Frye; Lisa Conner.

I deeply appreciate the quotes by Margaret E. Murie and the foreword by Bob Oakleaf, non-game coordinator for the Wyoming Game and Fish Department.

With her permission, I use a quotation of Mardy Murie's when admiring the Gray Jay. I am much honored. She and her late husband Olaus Murie are towering figures in 20th-century nature conservation and preservation, as well as in the art of living as intelligent, concerned, caring human beings.

Of course, there's Tom Mangelsen. He was willing to take the chance on a young kid with an idea for a book on birds that winter in the Northern Rocky Mountains. I, along with the likes of the National Geographic Society, public broadcasting systems worldwide and nature magazines galore, seek his delightful and insightful photography for my little project. Even at this very eventful period of his life, he obliges me. I am grateful to him.

And to you dear reader. Enjoy. Wear warm clothing.

Bert Raynes
Jackson Hole, Wyoming
2003

INTRODUCTION ↩

Winters are long in the Northern Rocky Mountains – long, severe and hard. Yet more than 120 different bird species remain there and survive through the frigid months.

In fact, winter never entirely leaves much of the region. Glaciers and snowfields are essentially permanent throughout the year. Below-freezing temperatures can occur on any day of the year, and they do occur commonly for much of the region that lies above 5,000 feet in elevation. Plant growing seasons end with the first hard frosts by September or October, not to resume until May or June of the following year – perhaps seven months later. Snowfall begins to accumulate by mid- to late October. Even at elevations below 5,000 feet or in sheltered valleys, winter is a six- or seven-month season.

Snow cover is early, deep and reluctant to yield. Ponds and small lakes can freeze over by November, creeks in December. Winter storms are frequent and can be harsh to the point of grimness. Prolonged cold temperatures ranging to –30°F, –50°F and even to –60°F occur and may persist for weeks. No relief as a result of moderating effects of the oceans reach the Northern Rockies. Challenges from winter's cold actually seem to intensify and compound. Nevertheless, these rigorous conditions are somehow endured by over-wintering birds and other animals.

Winter in the Northern Rocky Mountains has its own special beauty and appeal. However, it is also a demanding, relentless obstacle to each animal attempting to endure it.

It comes down to survival.

Life in the wild is never easy for any animal, for any bird. Life in the wild during winter becomes simply the essential task of searching for food. Unless enough food is found and consumed each day to sustain life through the winter night to follow, there is no further requirement to evade predators, avoid physical injury, elude hazards, find shelter. The focus must be on finding enough to eat.

In recognition of this overriding urgency, this book is organized around the kinds of foods and the various habitats which sustain those food sources in winter for birds to feed upon and utilize. Birds dependent upon these major food sources are illustrated and discussed briefly within each of these categories, viz.:

1. Wintering birds primarily dependent upon open water.
   For example: Waterfowl, Kingfisher, Ouzel.

2. Wintering birds primarily dependent upon buds, seeds and berries.
   For example: Ruffed Grouse, Red Crossbill, Horned Lark.

3. Wintering birds dependent on live prey, including insects.
   For example: Red-Tailed Hawk, Great Horned Owl.

4. Wintering birds that are omnivorous or eaters of carrion.
   For example: Black-Billed Magpie, Common Raven, Gray Jay.

Within these broad general categories, each bird employs differing strategies for its own winter survival. Of course, the fascination of bird study, of all natural history study, is the never-ending recognition of the wondrous ways nature has provided for all its creatures.

Half or more of the birds that nest in the Northern Rockies undertake yearly migrations, escaping winter and returning in spring or early summer. A bird in migration faces risks of injury, storm and, increasingly in our time, the discovery that its former destination no longer exists. A bird remaining in winter faces the rigors of intense cold, severe weather, and the possible failure of such food sources as seed crops or rodent populations. Tough choices. For birds, survival is a matter of strategy (read: instinct and learning) and luck.

Tom Mangelsen's photographs are featured in this book for an obvious reason: They're marvelous. I'm just fortunate he didn't have time to do the text, too, for he certainly could. Tom and I live in northwest Wyoming and share perhaps an insular notion that the Northern Rockies begin only a hundred miles south of Grand Teton National Park. In truth they extend south into northern Colorado and include Roosevelt and Arapaho national forests, the Medicine Bow Mountains and Rocky Mountain National Park. From there they trend north and northwesterly dividing the continent for some six hundred miles through Yellowstone National Park and Glacier National Park, and on up toward and beyond Banff and Jasper national parks in Alberta, Canada. They include the Wind River Mountains and the Snowy Range in Wyoming, the Bitterroots in Idaho and Montana, and the Lewis, Flathead and Selkirk mountains in Canada. The Bighorn Mountains in Wyoming and the Blue Mountains in Oregon are the outliers of the province. Elevations range from 3,500 feet to more than 14,000 feet. Numerous basins enclosed by or leading out of these mountain ranges are included within the Northern Rockies or Northern Montane geologic province. Major rivers head in the region whose wintering birds are highlighted here, rivers which run to the Pacific and Atlantic oceans, to the gulfs of Mexico and California, and to the Beaufort Sea and the Arctic Ocean.

This book is a celebration, an admiring acknowledgment of and to the birds of winter. Each bird that toughs it out each day throughout the Northern Rockies winter is an individual success. We salute each and every one.

Section 1

WINTERING BIRDS PRIMARILY DEPENDENT UPON OPEN WATER

Throughout even the coldest, harshest winter in the Northern Rockies, some waters remain open. Major rivers and some smaller streams remain ice-free, at least in stretches. Some large bodies of water seldom entirely freeze over, particularly some large lakes located west of the Continental Divide. There are also spring-fed creeks and thermal areas containing hot or warm bodies of open water and their runoffs.

These open waters are rich sources of various kinds of foods needed by many bird species. They host aquatic plants, fish and aquatic insects and insect larvae. Often their shorelines are snow-free and even unfrozen in spots, exposing seeds, terrestrial plants and those soft-bodied organisms certain birds probe for.

As a result, many birds survive by using these open waters. They move about as streams freeze or melt and as their food sources dwindle or flourish. This section of *Winter Wings* illustrates some of the species that are primarily dependent upon ice-free waters. Of course, other birds will use and be seen in the vicinity of their habitats.

When it comes to birds and their individual strategies with respect to ice-free waters, some like it hot, some like it swift, some like it deep. After all, birds are only human.

ᗒ TRUMPETER SWAN ᗕ
Cygnus buccinator

Trumpeter swans are breathtakingly beautiful birds, whether in flight or on the water. Once almost extirpated in the lower 48 states by hunting and habitat loss, an estimated 50 to 70 individuals survived as a restricted, essentially nonmigratory remnant population in and near Yellowstone National Park. They were able to persist on a few of Yellowstone's rivers where hot springs kept waters ice-free and because of the remoteness of the park's surroundings. They were joined in winter by the last Canadian trumpeters, survivors numbering perhaps 140. Any birds attempting to migrate farther south inevitably were destroyed.

It was touch and go for the great white birds. It still is, even though there are now nearly 4,000 trumpeter swans able to winter in the Northern Rockies outside of Alaska. Unless they can be restored to historic wintering areas, this is about the maximum number to be expected. In early winter, a small number of migrant trumpeter swans from Canada and Alaska join the resident population for a few weeks, along with migrating tundra (whistling) swans. Throughout the winter, trumpeters can be found on the Henry's Fork of the Snake and the Teton River in Idaho, in Yellowstone National Park, in Red Rocks National Wildlife Refuge in Montana and in Jackson Hole, Wyoming. Trumpeters are seldom found in winter north of Yellowstone.

✺ GREAT BLUE HERON ✺
Adrea herodias

Most of the great blue herons that nest in the Northern Rockies migrate by November, not to return until March. A few remain throughout the winter, however, always looking as if they wish they hadn't committed to staying.

They stand, shoulders drawn in, hunched over, moving as little as possible. They seem to be pretending for all the world that everything is hunky dory, like a high country fly fisherman on opening day for trout. Standing all day in frigid waters does tend to make one want to put his hands in his pockets and brood.

In late winter, spring migrant great blue herons begin to return and seem to perk up the stay-at-homes remarkably. By mid-March, generally, great blue herons will begin to revisit their nesting territories and explore reopening streams and ponds. After a few weeks, they seem to be happily and busily settled in once more, just the way they ought to be.

⤳ CANADA GOOSE ↶
Branta canadensis

The classic migration Canada geese pull off every fall is THE symbol of encroaching winter. Geese gather in ever-larger flocks during fall months, flying back and forth every day to feed and rest. Then something tells them to leave, right now, and they respond by flying south in noisy V's that waver across the orange sunsets and into the night, creating those scenes immemorially in paintings, photographs, documentaries and old timers' recollections. Winter comes, Canada geese leave. Everybody knows that.

So, what are they doing in the Northern Rockies during the worst days of winter?

They're neither sick nor injured; no frail bird survives these days, let alone many months of winter. It's possible they're from so far north they consider Glacier National Park or the Bitterroots to be the Deep South. More likely, these are individuals who enjoy winter, a white landscape and a chance to get the jump on future competitors for nesting sites come spring.

Canada geese nest by late March or early April in the Northern Rockies. What's half a year of freezing your feathers off with that prospect in mind? No big deal.

ᨠ MALLARD ᨠ
Anas platyrhynchos

The mallard is the most abundant and probably the best-known wild duck in the world. Males are grayish with a chestnut breast and sport a purple-blue speculum, or wing patch, bordered on each side with white. A glossy green head and narrow white neck collar distinguish these ducks from others. Females are a mottled brown with a whitish tail and dark bill.

In winter, many mallards go south only as far as necessary to find open water. As spring approaches, mallards return north as quickly as frozen waters reopen. These habitats almost assure that they can be encountered during the winter throughout the Northern Rocky Mountains. They'll be heard as well as seen, for mallards are noisy. Females make the familiar loud "quaack;" the male's voice is softer and higher in pitch. When annoyed or alarmed, however, the male will make a low, harsh note. Listen for it.

⨳ NORTHERN PINTAIL ⨳
Anas acuta

Although the majority of northern pintails tend to migrate to California in early autumn, a significant portion of their population seems to prefer to winter in the Northern Rockies. What's more, many of those pintails that do migrate often return north even while winter is still in full control of the region. This behavior qualifies them, in my judgment, as winter birds in the region.

On the water, northern pintails are elegant. The male is particularly striking, holding up his neck in a swan-like curve and his long, pointed tail upward at a rakish angle. Some old colloquial names indicate the appearance and attitude of the pintail: long neck; neck-twister; pheasant-duck; picket-tail; spike-tail; springtail.

In the air, northern pintails are fast, agile fliers, even for a large duck. Early nature writers called them the "greyhounds among waterfowl."

Many of those early nature writers tended to be close observers.

ᴥᴥ GADWALL ᴥᴥ
Anas strepera

Gadwalls are inconspicuous gray-brown ducks when sitting quietly and low in the water. In the air, however, a flashy white wing patch, located on the hind part of the wing, transforms the image from quiet and calm to one of vigorous action. Always a bit of a surprise for the bird watcher.

Gadwalls wintering in the Northern Rockies favor warm springs and spring creeks over big rivers. If winter is unusually severe, with below-average temperatures and little ice-free water, gadwalls will leave even the lowest elevations of the region, simply flying south far enough to find more suitable conditions. Once there, however, they tend to remain until about April. An entirely reasonable approach.

ꝯ BUFFLEHEAD ꝯ
Bucephala albeola

Buffleheads are dandy little birds. At a time in the brief history of the United States, when the comparison was more apparent and universally comprehensible than it is now, this duck was known as the "buffalo-headed duck." Its head, in fact, does appear disproportionately large for its body size, creating an illusion that buffleheads are smaller than their approximately foot-and-a-half length.

Bufflehead ducks tend to follow the 32°F temperature line in autumn and remain on open ponds and rivers throughout the Northern Rockies until deep winter sets in. Then they go south, not to reappear until spring is pretty well certain. None of this flying north during thaws or false springtime, a tactic some other ducks employ, only to have to retreat once more.

The bufflehead was once known as the "dipper-duck" because of the ease with which it can disappear under water. The "dipper" appellation has been dropped in reference to this duck, but remains appended to another dapper little bird, the water ouzel.

✢ COMMON GOLDENEYE ✢
Bucephala clanqula

The common goldeneye is nicknamed "the whistler" because of the unmistakable, characteristic, delightful sound this medium-sized duck's wings make in flight. Once learned, this wing song is forever familiar ... and helpful when goldeneyes fly high overhead at twilight or above an early morning winter fog.

The common goldeneye and its close relative, the barrow's goldeneye, are diving ducks that remain on mountain lakes until ice-up forces them to move to fast-flowing rivers and streams. These perky, hardy ducks can be found throughout the Northern Rockies region in winter, feeding in the rapids, diving under rim ice, and resting in sociable groups.

Male common goldeneyes are white-bodied with black on their backs, a large black head and a short neck. He has a round white spot between the bill and the eye, and his head is round as well. The female common goldeneye has a brown, round head and is overall a brownish gray.

ᘐ Barrow's Goldeneye ᘐ
Bucephala islandica

Barrow's goldeneye was once called the Rocky Mountain goldeneye because it is most abundant here. There is another breeding population in Labrador, but that need not concern us now.

The field marks of Barrow's goldeneye males are identical to those of the common goldeneye males – a white and black, medium-sized duck with a largish head. The male Barrow's largish head sports a crescent-shaped white spot in front of the eye, and the head is more triangular in shape than round. At close range and in good light, the male Barrow's goldeneye has a purplish sheen. The male common goldeneye will display a greenish gloss.

As spring approaches the female Barrow's goldeneye bill becomes yellow, an announcement welcomed by the males in her company, as well as by many human residents of the Northern Rockies.

✌ COMMON MERGANSER ✌
Mergus merganser

Here's a big, black and white duck, more than two feet in length. On the water, male common mergansers are quite rakish. Females have grayish bodies and crested rufous heads. In the air, mergansers fly with their heads, necks and bodies held in a straight line, seemingly straight arrows often flying in straight lines low and swift along a river's course.

Common mergansers are fish eaters and need a stretch of open water for takeoff. To survive winter in the Northern Rockies, they are mostly confined to big river systems or to large, unfrozen lakes. They seem reluctant to leave the region and have the habit of being among the first waterfowl to return north. As a result, a small but reliable number of common mergansers remain all winter long.

Field guides mention that this duck is not gregarious, to be found only in flocks of a few to perhaps two dozen individuals. However, this is not the experience of many an observer in the Northern Rockies, especially at winter's approach, when flocks of many hundreds assemble on lakes and rivers.

ᔓ **AMERICAN DIPPER** ᔓ
Cinclus mexicanus

American dippers live along and in the swift-flowing, riffle-filled streams of the mountain West. As winter clamps down on the Northern Rockies, these fascinating birds retreat only far enough to find ice-free, shallow flowing streams.

The American dipper, also well known as the water ouzel, is an utterly charming bird. But not because of its appearance; in fact, it's stubby, dark purplish-gray, short-tailed, rather unremarkable. It is, though, unmistakable in its behavior. For this is the odd little bird that casually walks into rushing streams, pokes about, submerges, pops up some little distance away, flying underwater or swimming on top. This is the bird that sings, cheerfully and tunefully, on −30°F winter mornings, that chases about a few inches above the surface of the waters. This is the bird that nonchalantly enters the water as if going into the drawing room after dinner for cigars and cognac, walks around a while, selecting an aquatic nymph here or there, and then reenters the world of the air never once appearing wet, cold or disheveled. Insouciance.

When momentarily occupying a rock, the dipper is in constant motion, doing knee bends. With each bob and clip, it closes its prominent nictitating membrane or third eyelid, which, being white, then draws your attention to the dipper's delicate, broken eye-ring.

⟡ Killdeer ⟡
Charadrius vociferus

Killdeer are hardy. Most killdeer that nest in the Northern Rockies make migrations only in winter to regions not far to their south. Even those travelers aren't usually gone more than a month or two. A few individuals stay the winter.

The killdeer gets its common name from the loud, articulated "killdee" cry, which it gives either in flight or from the ground. The call is often repeated almost to distraction – which is probably partly what it's about – and is given at any hour of day or night in summer. In winter the killdeer tends to be quiet. Maybe that's an energy-conservation thing; maybe it's a concentration on finding food. Maybe it's wondering what the rest of the gang might be doing down in Arizona or Texas or wherever.

Killdeer are dapper, long-legged, sleek, colorful shore birds. Alert, large-eyed, a pleasant olive-brown above, and white below. A close frontal view reveals four black bands, two prominent ones on the breast, two less noticeable ones on the head. In flight the bird's wings show a distinct white V stripe, and the rump is a distinctive bright orange-red brown. Nifty.

☙ BELTED KINGFISHER ❧
Ceryle alcyon

In the appropriate order of natural law as practiced by the preponderance of warm-bodied animals, males are more colorful, attractive, striking and handsome. Females, presumably for reasons pertaining to protection of the young, are relatively drab.

One exception to this elegant principle is demonstrated by the belted kingfisher; the female is more gaily colored than the male. Perhaps because the nest is in a burrow dug deep into a bank of the earth, the female can afford to gussy up. Not that the male isn't quite a dude; he's a foot-long, big-headed, stout-billed, bluish bird, sporting a shaggy head crest and a broad, gray-blue breast band across his white chest. Ah, but the lady has all of that plus an additional rusty breast band AND rust-brown flanks.

Kingfishers are closely linked to water. Throughout a Northern Rocky Mountain winter, lone belted kingfishers will be found wherever fishable, ice-free waters occur. To me, the call of the kingfisher, a series of rapid, unmusical notes quite like a rattle, is one of the premier wild sounds in nature. It's a pronouncement, a statement, defiance, a challenge…a jubilation.

Section 2

WINTERING BIRDS PRIMARILY DEPENDENT UPON SEEDS, BUDS AND BERRIES

At first thought one might conclude that any bird searching for seeds, cones and even berries could find them even in winter in the Northern Rocky Mountains. Broadly speaking that's true; yet these food sources are crops, the annual product of various plants. Thus, they are subject to fluctuations in supply and also in nutritive value. Moreover, in a heavy snow winter, or one in which occasional warm spells or strong winds fail to expose grasses and weeds, birds dependent upon these food sources must go elsewhere if they are to survive.

Birds described in this section move throughout the region's forests, across the prairies and ranch lands, or along the river bottom of their choice, searching for some item to eat. Not infrequently, birds of several species will be found foraging together, partly in competition, but more often pursuing their subtly separate survival strategies. Many of these species are readily attracted to seed feeders.

ꙅ Blue Grouse ꙅ
Dendragapus obscurus

Four true grouse and one other fowl-like species (the sage grouse) can be found in winter in the Northern Rockies. The two chosen for this book are the blue grouse and the ruffed grouse; they are the most familiar of the family to the observers. (The others are the spruce grouse and the sharp-tailed grouse.) All are big, plump birds and tasty, although the sage grouse is an acquired taste. The blue and ruffed grouse have, even to this day, little innate fear of humans; game laws fortunately have long been imposed on the taking of these birds, the "Fool Hens," or they might now be memories.

Blue grouse have dusky gray, almost black, tails with at most a thin band of light gray at the tip. Males are a uniform grayish or gray-brown and in the Northern Rockies sport dusky gray, almost black, tails that lack even a thin band of gray at their tips. Females are uniform gray-brown, speckled overall, and thus can be confused as ruffed grouse. Male courtship consists of a series of low, muffled, pulsing hoots, that are ventriloqual, difficult to pinpoint by us humans, that is; female grouse obviously have little difficulty.

꒰ RUFFED GROUSE ꒱
Bonasa umbellus

Another forest dweller, ruffed grouse indeed do have ruffs (and a slightly ruffed head), but the best bet is to look for their light, tan-colored tail with the distinctive black band near its tip. Males of each of these grouse spread their tails into splendid fans in courtship display, an activity engaged in increasingly when winter shows signs of giving way. Males also have an audible courtship display made by thumping their wings in and out, slowly accelerating beats, culminating in a whir. Humans can hear this "vocalization" if nearby, and sometimes can actually feel it in some fundamental way if at some distance.

In winter, ruffed grouse tend to move down into lower valleys, sheltered draws and brushy woodlands. Blue grouse, on the other hand, remain in coniferous and deciduous forests and actually tend to move up slope to uniformly coniferous zones. Each species depends upon buds and fruits throughout the winter.

⤳ Horned Lark ⤴
Eremophila alpestris

Horned larks help to fill those apparently barren places that stretch where trees don't grow but grasses, sagebrush, rabbitbrush and weeds do.

Horned larks flock to fill those empty vistas. Living in the open, searching for seeds, these small birds depend upon their numbers for security, distracting predators with coordinated group behavior. In winter, horned larks often forage the edges of highways for seeds and gravel; they fly up at the approach of your vehicle, settling again and yet again – to your dismay.

Watch these "road birds" fly up. Overhead, horned larks show black in their tails and fold in their wings between wing beats. They're only six or seven inches long, and overall a pinkish-brown. A close view reveals a prominent black crescent under each eye and a black kerchief over the breast. Then, of course, the horns: tufts of narrow, black feathers at each side of the back of the head, erectile according to mood, but erect often enough to give the bird its common name.

ꙮ STELLER'S JAY ꙮ
Cyanocitta stelleri

Because Steller's jays are omnivorous, they can, and do, remain within the coniferous forests of the Northern Rockies. Steller's jays readily take advantage of every food source that presents itself or can be found: pine nuts, weed seeds, beetles, a bit of grain here, a fruit or berry there.

These are fine-looking birds, displaying an unexpected range of colors from azure blue through black. Alert, saucy, sometimes silent and furtive, more often boldly noisy. All this plus a nifty, erectable crest.

The degree to which a Steller's jay's crest is elevated is an expression of its state of aggressiveness. You'd be justified in concluding that these jays go around pretty worked up most of the time. Sometimes their crests are fully elevated even when the birds fly around in the woods, and always when they are doing their golden eagle or red-tailed hawk cry imitation.

The male Steller's jay lowers his crest during his courtship of a female ... whereas many other males of many other species will puff themselves up during this activity.

Whatever works.

⊰ Gray Jay ⊱
Perisoreus canadensis

This permanent resident in the Northern Rockies was formerly named the Canada jay. It has also been called camp robber, venison bird, grease bird and, especially in the far North, Whiskey John. The native people called this bird wiss-ka-chon, "he who comes to your campfire." Margaret Murie recalls with pleasure the times she and her late husband, Olaus, spent in the bush with an Alaskan old timer who always added "shish," meaning small, diminutive. Whiskey John-Shish, little one who comes to the fire.

Gray jays are opportunist omnivores, skilled at sizing up human behavior and activity, including man's casual habit of waste disposal, and using them to advantage. It will snatch a bit of sandwich or plate of baked beans, a piece of bacon, almost anything edible thoughtlessly discarded or left unguarded. In return, it does offer a wink or nod in thanks.

But the gray jay is no full-time scrounger. In winter, it depends upon berries, insects, young fir needles and lichens. It's flat tough. So tough that it nests in late February and March when temperatures often still drop to −25°F and lower. Its young are among the first young birds to fledge in the Northern Rockies.

Young gray jays are slaty black, quite unlike the adults, which are – surprise! – gray. They have a white patch on their foreheads, and black patches on the backs of their heads – like a guy going bald. I have heard this jay likened to a big, slightly overgrown chickadee in appearance, but I don't see that.

Share a bit of lunch with a Whiskey John-Shish whenever you can. You'll both feel good about it.

♫ TOWNSEND'S SOLITAIRE ♫
Myadestes townsendi

Townsend's solitaires make vertical migrations from higher elevations to lower ones and back. Large numbers, no doubt a majority, move from the Northern Rockies to arid areas that support junipers and pinyon pine. But some individuals over-winter, often defending their territories, to be joined by early migrants before spring fully returns.

The Townsend's solitaire, a thrush, nests in the Rocky Mountains from above tree line down through the coniferous forests into wooded canyons. It is often overlooked but is actually widespread in occurrence. The solitaire's appearance and actions simply don't attract any attention, an undoubted advantage to the bird, if not to a hopeful observer.

It's a slim, dark gray bird, slender billed and, as with all the thrushes, large eyed. It has a white eye ring, white on each side of the tail, and orangish, buff colored wing patches. However, all of these field marks sound a lot more noticeable than they are.

Thrushes are songbirds. The Townsend's solitaire has a long, sweet, warbling song, which it will deliver at any season of the year. It's almost more of a delight to hear it in the middle of the day during the middle of winter than it is on a summer's day. But that's a close call.

☞ Clark's Nutcracker ☜
Nucifraga columbiana

Clark's nutcrackers are seed specialists. Their bills are tapered and flat at the ends and can easily and efficiently split open any pine or fir cone. Once a seed is partially open, the nutcracker can open its bill in a powerful gape and complete the shell opening. Meg Raynes calls it the original version of "the Jaws of Life."

Clark's nutcrackers have evolved a specialized, sub-lingual pouch that allows the bird to carry upwards of 90 pine seed kernels under its tongue, while leaving the bird free to hammer away, pull, examine, select or discard food – even to swallow a seed or some insect delicacy – and simultaneously to vocalize.

These rather handsome birds cache seeds for future use, carrying them and distributing them from their sub-lingual pouches to open places in the high elevations, where they bury them in groups of four to six or more. Locations are selected that are least likely to accumulate deep snow or that bare up during a thaw or in early spring. The birds have excellent memories, but inevitably some seeds go unutilized. Since they are bound to be viable seeds (the only ones the nutcracker will accept), if not eaten some likely will sprout. New stands of trees, and ultimately forests, result. This symbiotic relationship between selected conifers, principally white bark pine, and clark's nutcrackers has only recently been recognized.

Seed specialization notwithstanding, Clark's nutcrackers are ever ready to pick up an unwary vole or mouse as a tasty morsel.

❧ RED-BREASTED NUTHATCH ❧
Sitta canadensis

The red-breasted nuthatch's fortune is tied closely to the pine seed crop of each year. If the crop is good, this nuthatch remains in winter within the coniferous forests of the Northern Rockies. If not, it makes southerly movements in search of food, often traveling in large numbers.

The red-breasted is smaller than its relative, the white-breasted nuthatch, averaging around 4 1/2 inches in length. Of course, its under parts are washed with a rust color, back and wings a bluish-gray, a black cap on the head, a white line over the eye, a black line through the eye. Attractive.

This bird is so small that it can be overlooked, and often would be if it didn't have the habit of frequently uttering its note as it goes busily about important business. Its note is a high-pitched nasal "ank," like that of a little tin horn, audible at considerable distance.

Red-breasted nuthatches are acrobatic, climbing up or down the trunks and over branches of coniferous trees. In this hyperactivity and in winter, it is often found in the company of chickadees, perhaps a downy woodpecker or a few golden kinglets. It's nice to have company on a wintry day.

☞ White-Breasted Nuthatch ☜
Sitta carolinensis

The white-breasted nuthatch is essentially nonmigratory, opting to remain in or near its home territory all year. It prefers a mixed deciduous-conifer forest, especially deciduous trees; in the Northern Rockies this implies lower elevations, foothills, riparian areas. It avoids rangeland and higher peaks.

No one will fail to notice the white-breasted nuthatch's disposition to go head first down tree trunks or down a rock face in its search for eggs of pupae and hibernating insects. Chickadees can hang upside down; nuthatches can run down a tree trunk.

This is a sturdy little bird, only six inches long. It has a pointed bill and a stubby tail. It's plain and bluish-gray above and – big surprise – white-breasted.

But, you never know: The moniker "Nuthatch" implies an ability to open the shells of hard nuts, which it normally cannot. Its short tail doesn't offer the bird sufficient leverage for that task. Nuthatches can and do, however, force soft-shelled nuts and seeds into crevices in tree barks, and then have at them.

The word "cute" suggests itself.

ꕔ BOHEMIAN WAXWING / CEDAR WAXWING ꕔ
Bombycilla garrulus/Bombycilla cedrorum

Cedar waxwings are resident in the Northern Rockies, nesting as far north, in fact, as Canada's Northwest Territories. Bohemian waxwings nest even farther north, to the vicinity of the Arctic and Bering seas.

Both species tend to be wanderers, searching for fruits, fresh or dried: crabapples, rose hips, cedar and juniper berries, hawthorn, mountain ash and the like. In winter, they travel in flocks, often large ones not infrequently comprised of members of each species, remaining in one area until the food supply runs low, moving on and on yet again.

Many generations of waxwings ago, I read a description of the cedar waxwing that impressed me for its old-fashioned flowery style and accuracy:

> *"Who can describe the marvelous beauty and elegance of this bird? What other dressed in a robe of such delicate beauty and silky texture? Those shades of blending beauty, velvety black, shifting saffrons, Quaker drabs, pale blue and slate trimmings of white and golden yellow, and the little red appendages on the wing, not found in any other family of birds, all combined with its graceful form, give the bird an appearance of elegance and distinction peculiarly its own."*
> 　　　　　　　　　　　　　　　　　　　　　　　　　　-E. H. Forbush

Yeah, but they don't sing well.

Neither do their larger cousins, the bohemian waxwings. However they have pretty much all of the above, plus rusty, salmon-colored under-tail coverts, and white and yellow wing markings.

⤳ EVENING GROSBEAK ↢
Coccothraustes vespertinus

It's not called a grosbeak without cause. Evening grosbeaks do indeed have large bills. Conical bills, bordering on comical. Imposing bills. Bills quite obviously capable of cracking seeds.

As winter approaches, evening grosbeaks gather into sociable flocks, leaving their boreal forest nesting grounds to wander throughout the Northern Rockies in search of trees and shrubs bearing suitable seeds and berries.

Male evening grosbeaks are a burnished deep yellow with a dark head, a yellow eyebrow and a black and white forked tail. And that beak: Not only big, it ranges from a pale yellowish to a pale greenish in color. Female evening grosbeaks are silver-grayish but otherwise similarly marked. On first meeting the bird, lots of folks think perhaps it is some misplaced or erratic, lost, exotic parrot.

Fortunately for all of us, evening grosbeaks are regular wintering and sometimes summering birds of the region. They have become acquainted with bird feeding stations where a troop of these gregarious birds, only eight inches long, quite astonish by the quantity of seeds that they can consume, all the while chattering away or making loud, ringing, two-note whistles. Rather like a grade school cafeteria, or a senior center dining area.

⟿ PINE GROSBEAK ⟿
Pinicola enucleator

The pine grosbeak actually isn't a grosbeak; it's a finch. It isn't restricted entirely to pine trees but, it is an attractive songbird, pleasant to look upon, listen to, know.

Pine grosbeaks are robin-sized (by the way reader, just about half of the land birds in North America are the robin length of 10 inches in length or shorter, which is one reason hackneyed natural history writers, like me, refer so often to robins when considering a bird's size). In any event, male pine grosbeaks are not only robin-sized, but they also resemble robins in that they are pale red and gray in plumage and have long tails. Pine grosbeaks have short, thick bills, quite unlike the sharp, pointed bills robins have … Okay, okay; the resemblance isn't all that close after all.

Pine grosbeaks are erratic in distribution during winter. They wander in search of seeds and fruits, usually remaining within the mixed deciduous and coniferous forests of the Northern Rockies. In some winters they must flare out to lower elevations and even to the Great Plains. They are relatively unafraid of man and often can be approached closely. In parts of Canada, the pine grosbeak was once familiarly known as "the mope." Fittingly, for it often will sit quietly and move slowly and deliberately. This behavior is sometimes described as "tame."

⨪ DARK-EYED JUNCO ⨪
Junco hyemalis

Juncoes likely to be found in winter in the Northern Rockies – or for that matter, at any time of the year – will have dark eyes. Not long ago, juncoes considered as separate types flew around as Oregon juncoes, slate-colored juncoes or gray-headed juncoes until they suddenly were given the awkward name of dark-eyed junco. This desperate move may have satisfied the taxonomists, but I think it has cost some bird watchers the reward of making appropriate field identifications; wise watchers will still try to discriminate.

Male dark-eyed juncoes are unstriped, dark gray and white, dapper little (six-inch) birds. White outer tail feathers flash as the bird feeds on wild seeds and fruits, and show prominently as it flutters away. Many juncoes go south to escape winter, earning the familiar nickname of "snowbird," used now to describe people who do the same.

Birdwatchers in the Northern Rocky Mountains during winter are fortunate to relax in the knowledge that they are unlikely to come across one of those yellow-eyed junco devils who live in the Southwest. What a load off their minds.

ꝏ PINE SISKIN ꝏ
Carduelis pinus

An old name for this diminutive finch (only 4 1/2 to 5 inches in length) was the Northern canary. It might also have been called the Evergreen Mountain Forest Bird, for it feeds mostly on the seeds of conifers, a source available in winter throughout the Northern Rockies.

Hardy, widespread, but erratic in occurrence, the pine siskin is seldom lonely. Social, not only with its kind, but also not infrequently found in the company of goldfinches, crossbills and redpolls. Their call note is a helpful distinctive wheezy "chee-ee", quite useful in their identification and often given by the majority of pine siskins in the group. Other notes are sweet, resembling those of tame canaries, goldfinches and other finches.

The pine siskin is a generally tame bird, but surprisingly aggressive when feeding. At a feeder it often fends off much larger birds. Pine siskins are dark above and on the wings, and are heavily streaked. Touches of yellow give contrast to the wings and rump.

Note: Tom Mangelsen informs that he once harbored a pine siskin with appropriate sanction, and it became a favorite. Yup, every opportunity to observe closely and at length the behavior of a bird or other animal is deeply rewarding.

⇝ CASSIN'S FINCH ⇜
Carpodacus cassinii

Cassin's finches breed in the coniferous forests of the high mountains of the Northern Rockies. Families form flocks and remain in the higher elevations until about mid-winter, when a general southerly and downslope migration takes place.

Male and female Cassin's finches differ distinctly in appearance. Females (and immatures) are brown, heavily striped, sparrow-like birds. They have quite long tails for their six-inch length, tails that are slightly notched. Males have clear, pinkish breasts, pink also on their bellies and flanks, and a jaunty red crown patch that contrasts well with a brownish back.

Where Cassin's finches overlap in range with the house finch and purple finch, species to which they are closely related, it is a pleasant task to try to figure out just which one is in your view. Pleasant, but somewhat frustrating, even when dealing with males. The best way to discriminate among the females is to decide which male species she is hanging out with.

I particularly enjoy listening to Cassin's finches. Their song lifts my spirits. Oh, I recognize that's not why they sing, and I accept that as a charter member of the Jackson Hole Deaf-As-A-Post Lunch Bunch, I may miss some individual notes, lose a phrase perhaps; yet they do sing to me.

I hope they will sing to you.

ᴈ GRAY-CROWNED ROSY FINCH/BLACK ROSY FINCH ᴈ
Leucosticte tephrocotis/Leucosticte atrata

Winter brings rosy finches down from the timberline of the high mountains of the Northern Rockies to the valleys and onto the basins and plains in search of seeds and occasional insects.

In winter, rosy finches frequently gather in flocks of hundreds of birds. To see a large, closely knit flock of these brownish-blackish-gray birds whirl into the air only to land for a few moments of restless feeding, picking up gravel and walking about before taking off once again, is still another seasonal delight. See and hear as well, for these bouncy, sparrow-sized finches tend to keep up an almost constant cheerful twittering.

"Rosy finch" was the overall name recently used to include individuals formerly known as gray-crowned rosy finch, black rosy finch and brown rosy finch, denying them distinct species identification. As a bird watcher, I regretted this "lumping together" because it tended to make a winter watcher inattentive to wonderful details. It is nice to see these birds now returned to their proper status.

The gray-crowned rosy finch has a brownish body, a sporty gray patch on the back of the head and a pinkish wash on the wings. As it comes into late winter and spring plumage, the black rosy finch shows a distinctly blackish body and back, a gray head band and much pink on wings and belly. The brown rosy finch has, as you can guess, a brownish head with no gray.

✍ RED CROSSBILL ✍
Loxia curvirostra

Red crossbills nest early and nest late; in some parts of the Northern Rockies, they nest any time from March into December. Then they wander unpredictably through coniferous forests. You just never know when you're going to come across a little band or perhaps a modest flock of them.

Red crossbills hatch and fledge with uncrossed bills, but their long, narrow mandibles are adapted to extract seeds from pinecones. Crossbills insert their crossed bills into an interstice of a pinecone, then open those mandibles, removing scales and exposing seeds quicker than it takes to read about it.

Crossbills also possess a peculiar scoop-shaped tongue that gathers seeds in and a throat pouch that can store, at least temporarily, a handful of seeds.

On top of all that, male red crossbills are an unusual red, a dull yet somehow glowing red. Females are a dull olive gray with a yellowish rump and breast.

Red crossbills are inordinately fond of salt and go to the edges of highways, on which salt is so unfortunately wantonly and ignorantly spread, to obtain it. Many are killed by motor vehicles while in this pursuit, compounding the overall foolishness.

❧ Northern Flicker ❧
Colaptes auratus

It can't be a simple matter for a bird that eats ants as its most important food, and thus commonly feeds on the ground, to make a living in a Northern Rockies winter. Yet a few northern flickers manage it, retreating to riparian habitats and deciduous woods to find insects, berries or fruits.

Flickers are handsome, good-sized, and up to 14 inches long. They have brown backs and tan chests with a black patch displayed across it in the fashion of a kerchief. They make deeply undulating, bouncy passages through the air, and if heading away from your position, they display a conspicuous white rump patch. They really flip the bird.

Two forms of the northern flicker are found in the Northern Rockies, and sometimes hybrids of the two are discernible. Flight and tail feathers of the red-shafted form are – you guessed it – a rich salmon red; in the yellow-shafted type, they're what you'd think. The red-shafted flicker predominates in the West.

Bright-colored feathers of these flashy birds are among a selected few kinds appreciated, even revered, by some Native Americans who often incorporated them into a variety of artifacts ranging from clothing to adornment and weaponry. They look pretty good on the living bird, too.

✢ Common Redpoll ✢
Carduelis flammea

Common redpolls possess about all the traits a bird needs to have to survive cold weather. In fact, they can take about the coldest temperatures any songbird is known to withstand. Redpolls nest in the Far North, and if seeds and buds upon which they depend are in good supply, they remain there all year. They may avoid the risks of migration that way, but instead they must be able to live through nights which can last 18 to 20 hours. That's a long time for any bird to survive when temperatures may be −40°F to −50°F or lower, even through shivering or by becoming temporarily torpid.

What common redpolls (and crossbills, too, actually) have is a little pocket halfway down their esophagus into which they store seeds they stock up on before retiring and which they, well, "snack on" throughout the night hours.

Common redpolls sport a red or orange-red "poll" or cap on their foreheads. Otherwise they are small, streaked gray-brown birds with small but distinctive black chin marks. Males have rosy breasts and sides. Despite the redpoll and the chin mark, these finches are so similar to the pine siskins and American goldfinches that they can be easily overlooked. They deserve recognition; any common redpolls that turn up in the Northern Rockies have come quite a long way, and it's the hospitable thing for us to do.

꒰ SNOW BUNTING ꒱
Plectrophenax nivalis

Snow buntings nest in the treeless tundra of the Arctic and sub-Arctic regions and come south in winter to find grass and weed seeds not covered by snow. Those that come to the greater Northern Rocky Mountain regions will be found along road edges and on open steppes and ranches.

Concerning snow buntings, naturalist John Burroughs wrote, "The only one of our winter birds that really seems a part of winter, that seems to be born of the whirling snow, and to be happiest when storms drive thickest and coldest, is the snow bunting, the real snowbird, with plumage copied from the fields where the drifts hide all but the tops of the tallest weeds, large spaces of pure white touched here and there with black and gray and brown." *

Yes, John.

Sure enough, the birds themselves in winter are in fact black and gray and brown. Brown on the head, black on the wings and tail, brown and white on underparts. Overhead, snow buntings appear almost entirely white. A part of winter.

* *Far and Near*, by John Burroughs, 1904, Houghton-Mifflin Co., N.Y.

꒰ AMERICAN GOLDFINCH ꒱
Carduelis tristis

Perhaps no other bird surprises an observer during a Northern Rockies winter than the American goldfinch. The "wild canary" is associated in one's mind's eye with full summer, even late summer, and not with winter. It is, however, a year-round resident that travels erratically in winter in search of seed-bearing plants left uncovered by the snow or, alternatively, in coniferous forests.

A bright yellow little bird with black wings and tail is almost universally recognized as the American goldfinch. As winter approaches, however, male goldfinch turn an overall dull olive color, and the females and immatures often puzzle an observer who "can't find them anywhere in my bird book."

The American goldfinch is one bird species that probably has benefited from the happy habit many people enjoy of supplementary feeding birds. Moreover, the Northern Rockies has been one of the few beneficiaries of a significant increase in the region of several exotic thistle species, which responded to the warm, dry weather pattern witnessed in the 1980s and early 1990s. An old common name for the goldfinch was "thistle bird," and for reason; goldfinch are late nesters, timing their nesting to the blooming and going-to-seed of thistles.

As winter begins to wane, male goldfinch become increasingly bright yellow, just about the tempo at which daylight hours increase. Or so I'd like to believe.

Section 3

WINTERING BIRDS DEPENDENT UPON LIVE PREY, INCLUDING INSECTS

Birds that hunt live prey in order to survive, and birds that eat flying insects or various small mammals or other birds, face a sharp decrease in the sources and abundance of their food as the Northern Rockies winter arrives. In response, many of these hunters choose to migrate, ultimately following the flycatchers, tanagers, swallows and other bird families that must migrate.

Observers of the natural history of the region often remark that predators such as an occasional red-tailed hawk will linger as winter arrives and will stay if prey remains available. Some rough-legged hawks that come to the Rockies from the Arctic tundra to winter will also stay unless forced to go farther south or east to find food. Therefore, some of the birds described in this section may be absent in some winters, but common in others.

I have included chickadees and woodpeckers in this category because their major dependence in winter is on finding the larvae, egg cases and hibernating adults of insects, and not upon the occasional seed or bud they also consume.

ᔥ MOUNTAIN CHICKADEE / BLACK-CAPPED CHICKADEE ᔥ
Poecile gambeli/Poecile atricapilla

It's a temptation to say that chickadees are everybody's favorite bird. For me – every bird, any bird, each bird – is my favorite when I'm looking at it, or thinking about it. I'd bet, though, that chickadees are the immediate favorite of anyone who's been out on a blustery Northern Rockies winter day long enough to have become even a bit weary and dispirited, and is suddenly joined by a merry little band of mountain and black-capped chickadees. Their energetic bouncing through the shrubs and trees; their jaunty little lisping call notes directed – could it be? – at him; their inquisitive, accepting glances; their companionship. What a lift.

Yet another charming characteristic of chickadees is their early recognition of the lengthening of daylight hours immediately after the winter solstice in late December, so that by early January, given a sunshine-filled hour, these frisky little tykes will whistle their spring notes. Oh Joy! Oh Promise!

Mountain and black-capped chickadees each, in fact, have black caps. A white line, however, through the black cap over the eye identifies the mountain. Another species, the boreal chickadee, is found within the northern limits of the Northern Rocky Mountain region; it has a dull brown cap and distinctly brown flanks. All chickadees are small, plump, acrobatic, pleasing and companionable birds.

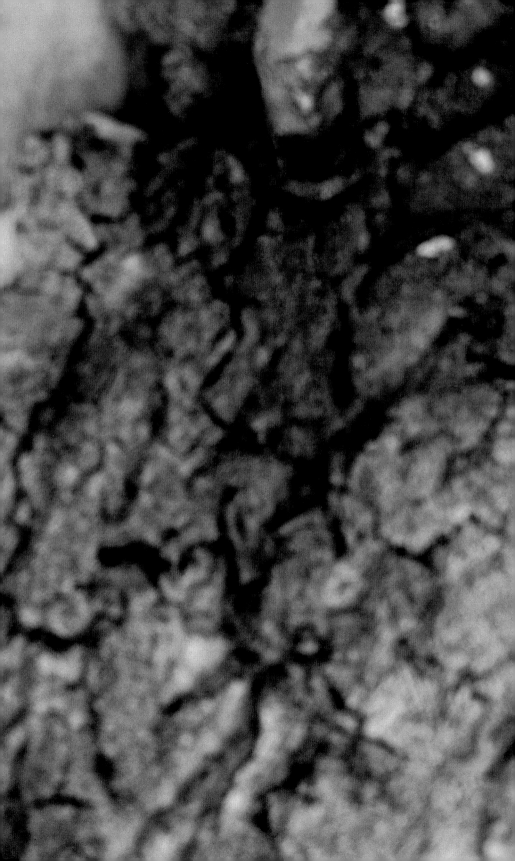

ᘒ NORTHERN SHRIKE ᘓ
Lanius excubitor

Small numbers of northern shrikes ordinarily over-winter in the Northern Rockies; about every four years, almost surely in response to the corresponding cycle in mouse populations in western Canada and Alaska, far larger numbers occur. They hunt forest openings, willow- and shrub-bordered riparian areas, and from fence lines of farms and ranches.

Their prey, small mammals and birds in winter plus large insects and reptiles in other seasons, is regularly impaled on thorns, twigs, barbed wire or wedged in some secure fashion. Ordinarily, the prey is then consumed, in whole or part. However, there are other purposes for this unusual habit: Male shrikes engaged in courtship and territorial display will hang some prey out as enticements in demonstrations of hunting skills. These latter functions are more typical in spring and summer, for it pays to advertise.

This habit of hanging prey carcasses about on hooks attracts shrike females, one may be sure. People have noticed, too, earning this species the nickname "butcher bird." Shrikes are sleek birds, as you would expect of a bird of prey. Gray, white and black, the black on the head creating a mask that does not meet over the bill. The lower mandible is pale, the upper mandible is black. Black wings are spotted with white, black tail bordered irregularly in white.

Although robin-sized, it appears larger and is huskier, and somehow fashionably attired.

❧ Song Sparrow ❧
Melospiza melodia

Early names given this bird by white settlers in North America included "Silver Tongue" and "Everybody's Darling." Descriptions went along the lines of "a sweet singer of the spring and summer, and a useful friend the year round."

What is there to add to that?

Perhaps a word or two. The song sparrow's song is also occasionally given in winter when it seems just to burst forth. It's highly variable and there are many local dialects, but it almost always begins with two to four clear notes on one pitch, followed by a cheerful mixture of musical and buzzy notes.

The song is most often delivered as the bird perches on the very top of a shrub or post. Look for six-inch-long finches whose heavy breast streaks converge into a dark central breast spot. The tail is long and rounded, and is pumped up and down as the bird flutters off. "Sparrow" literally means "flutterer."

Song sparrows utilize a wide variety of habitats in winter, and thus can be found in most winters even during harsh conditions. Sustained cold temperatures below 10°F eventually force song sparrows to withdraw, but they will return at the first hint of milder conditions.

↝ HAIRY WOODPECKER / DOWNY WOODPECKER ↜
Picoides villosus/Picoides pubescens

That the downy and hairy woodpeckers are related is apparent. The hairy looks to be a bigger version of the downy. That they have evolved as separate species indicates that each successfully occupies a separate and distinct niche in nature.

One small aspect of this distinction may be more easily observed in winter than in summer. Although both woodpecker species subsist by searching out and extracting the larvae of boring beetles from live and dead wood, downy woodpeckers are also small enough to feed upon gall insects found on larger nonwoody plants, while their bigger cousins cannot.

In winter in the Northern Rockies, both of these species make elevation migrations, moving gradually downslope through the forests. A few not infrequently come into the cities and towns and farms.

These sturdy birds are white with black on their backs, wings and tails. The white on the back is always visible on the bird, whether perched or in flight, making it a good field mark. The hairy woodpecker is about 10 inches long, and its bill is about as long as the diameter of its head; the downy's bill seems small for the size of the bird's head, and the bird is only about six inches long.

By late February these woodpeckers will be joyfully paired off in noisy, showy courtship that livens the depths of winter and offers hope for spring. Your basic Rocky Mountain relationship.

✍ RED-TAILED HAWK ✍
Buteo jamaicensis

A little tip: Red-tailed hawks hunt by day in the same habitat that great horned owls hunt by night.

The red-tailed hawk is a large, broad-winged soaring hawk, with some females reaching two feet in length. The relatively short, wide tail is usually reddish – what did you expect? – but usually only on its upper surface. Below, the tail is often pale brownish-gray but often hints at red. Red-tails, however, can vary greatly in plumage from very pale to dark brown to blackish individuals. Indeed, some birds don't have red tails but overall grayish ones instead. These adept predators often perch at the very top of a tree or similar vantage point, quite conspicuously, as they search for their mammalian prey.

Red-tailed hawks are common in the Rockies in summer, but in winter most retreat from the highest elevations; many migrate long distances. But except in the most extreme winters red-tails will be found, often near roadsides where small mammals seek warmth.

❧ COMMON SNIPE ❧
Gallinago gallinago

That a few common snipe choose to winter in the Northern Rockies is a bit of a surprise. That's because their major food consists of worms, small crustaceans and invertebrates for which they probe in mud. Even when taking berries or seeds, they seldom are found other than in wetlands. Unfrozen wetlands.

The common snipe's plumage permits it to be well camouflaged in marches, bogs or along stream edges. At one's approach it will ordinarily "freeze" in place, hoping to remain undetected. When it decides it must flee, it launches as if it were a jet fighter propelled from an aircraft carrier. It makes a raspy "jaack" utterance, much like an oath, and zigzags erratically off, staying low to the earth before dropping back into another hiding place.

Common snipe that do migrate return north early, as more and more ground begins to thaw. They soon become "fence-post birds," not infrequently plopped right on the most photogenic post in sight, calmly surveying the landscape and sky, probably waiting for a friendly bird watcher or photographer.

ᴿᴼ ROUGH-LEGGED HAWK ᴿᴼ
Buteo lagopus

Rough-legged hawks nest so far north, in the Arctic actually, that they appear to consider any place below the Canadian-United States border to be the Deep South. Open range within and adjacent to the Northern Rockies looks good to them, and some arrive as early as October. The south wears thin by the beginning of March, when they begin their spring migration.

Seen from underneath, light-phase birds of this buteo species display long wings with prominent dark "wrist patches," a broad band of dark across the belly and a black band at the tip of the tail. Dark-phase rough-legs have black bodies and underwings against which white flight and undertail feathers are highlighted.

Seen perched on a fence post surveying the terrain for small mammals, the rough-legged hawk appears bulky and shows a white tail bordered in black in light-phase individuals. Oh, yes: The legs are indeed feathered clear down to the foot.

Rough-legged hawks hunt in the gray fog of winter mornings and during the gathering evening dusk. Company on your outings and commutes.

⤳ GREAT HORNED OWL ⤶
Bubo virginianus

Winter strategy: Oh, you know, sit around all day in a tree somewhere, and snooze. Come late afternoon, go hunting. Look for squirrels, muskrats, mice, perhaps a cat or porcupine, for birds of almost any size, including smaller owls, maybe a fish or even a skunk. Come January, get turned on. Talk all night ... sweet talk. Court your mate. Get ready to nest by late January or February by setting into an old red-tailed hawk's nest or similar ready-made quarters. More all-night conversations ... pillow talk, but two eggs will usually satisfy. Hunt for two, then for four. Time passes.

Authorities and casual observers alike agree that the great horned owl is the fiercest and most powerful of North American owls. "The Tiger of the Air" was an early moniker, in recognition of its strength, hunting prowess, presence and austerely regal appearance.

The "horns" of course are feathers, fully two inches long. The owl normally holds them erect but will tilt them backward when angered. The winged tiger indeed.

Oops, did I just write that a bird could be "angry?" Isn't that hopelessly anthropomorphic? You bet.

⌇ NORTHERN SAW-WHET OWL / NORTHERN PYGMY OWL ⌇
Aegolius acadicus/Glaucidium gnoma

The northern saw-whet owl and the northern pygmy owl are two of the small owls of the Northern Rocky Mountain regime. Each is barely larger than a large sparrow when full grown, but don't let their small size deceive. Each is among the most aggressive of predators.

Owls can be difficult to see, for it's often to their advantage in hunting – or being hunted – to be unobserved. However, these two little owls are largely diurnal, making your chance better. Often passerine birds discover them and "mob" these owls to warn unsuspecting potential victims and drive these owls away. Go to the scene and direct your attention to the focus of the activity.

Owl calls also can help locate these attractive birds, and each species can call all year long, but particularly in mid- and late winter. The saw-whet often emits its soft note in seemingly endless, rapid succession. The pygmy owl's call is a single, slower note, given every two to three seconds.

To top it off, these tiny owls are charmingly photogenic. The saw-whet looks out from a tree cavity with solemn eyes or with its head at some impossible angle. The pygmy owl poses with its tail angled to its body or displaying the unusual pattern on the back of its head, one that resembles the beak and eyes of another owl's face.

ᴔᴑ GREAT GRAY OWL ᴑᴣ
Strix nebulosa

The great gray owl depends upon rodents, particularly, pocket gophers, mice and voles. Yet it doesn't like to leave the comfort of heavy timber. Solution? Hunt open meadows and hillsides from big trees. About what you would do under the circumstances.

The great gray owl prefers to hunt by day, especially during late afternoon and twilight hours. It has excellent vision and often uses that sense preferentially to its hearing for prey location. This is counter to the strategy used by most owl species (and a bit of an advantage to the wildlife observer seeking wintering animals).

Although great gray owls are not abundant in the Northern Rockies, winter or summer, there are more than had been thought a decade or so ago. They occur down the spine of the Northern Rockies and across the breadth of the North Montane Province. At 24 to 33 inches, the great gray is the largest North American owl; this dimension includes its very long tail (about 10 inches in length). It is smoothly round-headed, has prominent facial disks, yellow eyes and a pronounced white moustache over a dark goatee. Unforgettable.

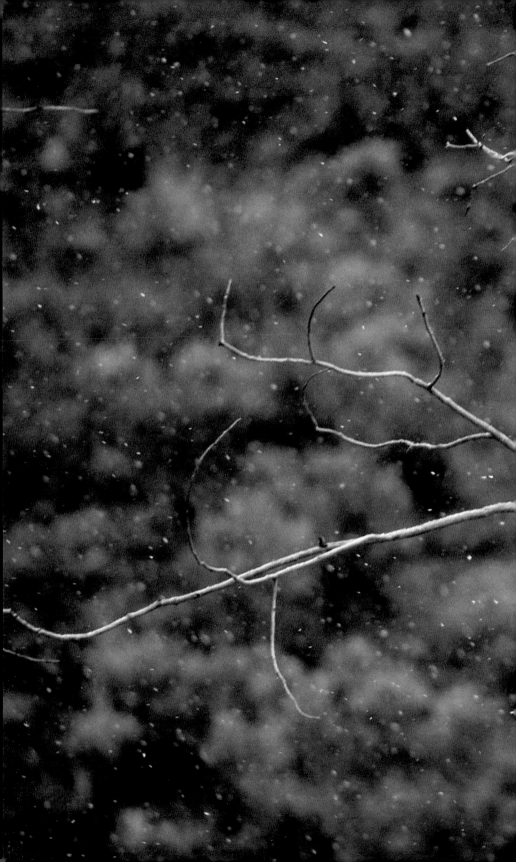

SECTION 4

WINTERING BIRDS THAT ARE OMNIVOROUS OR EATERS OF CARRION

A bird able to utilize a variety of food sources increases its chances for survival. Should one source fail, others may yet be found. A bald eagle whose stretch of river freezes over, depriving it of fish, can hunt small mammals and will search for carrion. Common ravens follow game herds, patrol highways, frequent landfills, scout for discards in cities, towns and around farm and ranch buildings.

There is a certain amount of arbitrariness in choosing the particular birds included in this section. Bald and golden eagles, strictly speaking, aren't omnivorous, because they don't eat vegetable matter, but their dependence in many winters upon carrion is sometimes complete for extended periods.

ᕗ GOLDEN EAGLE ᕘ
Aquila chrysaetos

For much of the year, golden eagles and bald eagles occupy different habitats. Golden eagles are at home in the highest mountains and in the arid basins of the Northern Rockies. Bald eagles prefer riparian terrain.

In winter, however, both eagle species hunt the same general territory. Golden eagles are perhaps the more opportunistic of the two and possibly the more aggressive.

A bit of art is required – or the need for practice – to distinguish every golden from every bald eagle. Each is a burly bird, broad and long of wing, unmistakably large. Golden eagles are dark on body and on tail. The crown of the head and nape of the neck are blond or a pale gold; in some lighting conditions, and on some golden eagles, these blond or gold feathers may make the head appear as white as the white of the bald eagle head feathers. On mature eagles, one can check for tail color. Black means a golden, white says a bald.

That was easy. Now then, as to immature eagles … immature eagles can be readily confusing. I recommend a good field guide.

⤳ BALD EAGLE ⇌
Haliaeetus leucocephalus

The bald eagle's winter strategy is appropriately straightforward. In the Northern Rockies that means following the river systems to where fish are spawning or available, following ungulate migrations, going to locations where motor vehicles are the killers that don't consume their quarry. If that doesn't work out, remove to the seacoast for a couple of months.

Bald eagles seem to have an innate ability to select the photographically correct (p.c., that is) snag of the grandest tree in sight to perch upon; know how best to present a winning profile; and to choose just which sector of sky to soar gracefully within.

All well and good. But go out on a blustery day, when the snow stings your face and batters your eyes and your inclination is to find shelter, and watch a bald eagle out exercising its control of flight in a combination of flight mastery and hunting skill. Eagle essence.

I wonder sometimes that Ben Franklin never noticed that side of the bald eagle (but if so, it's one of the very few things he missed) because he concentrated on its being a bully and an eater of carrion. I believe the bald eagle simply knows its capabilities and its limitation and is content. Not a bad idea for a national symbol.

⚡ Black-Billed Magpie ⚡
Pica pica

It's tempting to remark that no other bird in and near the Northern Rockies resembles the black-billed magpie. Nor, for that matter, in North America. Two caveats to that notion. One is that there is a yellow-billed magpie in California. The other is that the magpie often somehow contrives to look like some other species on many occasions and can be deceiving. One simply doesn't at first expect cryptic attributes in a big, black and white, 20-inch-long bird, fully half of which is a distinctively wedge-shaped tail. Nevertheless, a black-billed magpie facing you from a fence post at some distance, or half concealed in a clump of willows, or sitting on the tip of a fir tree or barn roof, can at first glance be thought to be somebody else – a common raven, say, or a clark's nutcracker, even perhaps a hawk or owl.

In flight, this species is not often mistaken: a flickering, periodic wingbeat sequence, a stroboscopic black/white/black flashing of the wings, a swooping and banking, the exaggerated long tail, all almost shout "magpie!"

The black-billed magpie is a bird of the arteries of the Northern Rockies, found along the highways and byways, streams, rivers, irrigation ditches, in pastures, around ranches and farms and in towns. Far more than most birds, it is adaptable and clever, capable of hunting insects and rodents, content with carrion. It is found from the lowest elevations to more than 8,000 feet. A familiar bird, which does not deserve the disdain familiarity tends to bring.

⇝ Common Raven ⇜
Corvus corax

Anywhere you can go, common ravens can, too. They can go higher than you can go – even if you stand on the highest peak in the Northern Rockies. Anything you can eat, ravens can, too. In fact, it's highly likely they can fly better than you can; however, you probably do have a more exciting nightlife. Moreover, don't look for ravens when spelunking.

The raven is just fun to watch. On the ground, it's kind of measured and stately when walking, awkward when hopping. In the air, the raven is capable of slow measured flight, rapid deliberate flight, of soaring and sailing and of spectacular aerobatics. Ravens often ride in a thermal or a gale, apparently for fun. They will spiral in groups above the carrion. They will often swoop and coast, and can dive with closed wings, barrel roll or spin.

Especially in spring, and especially in courtship flights, ravens will twist, roll over sideways, chase each other, turn somersaults, soar wingtip to wingtip, even touch wingtips while one of the pair flies upside down.

Sometimes, also for fun, ravens will pick on hawks and even eagles and generally put them to rout. It's not fun for a hawk to have a half-dozen ravens bullying him. It's not fun either for a raven to be mobbed by blackbirds whenever he flies over during their nesting time.

Watch the ravens now and then, listen to their loud, hoarse call note, or their deep grunt, or their deep, bell-like tones or creaks or croaks. Look at a pair of ravens sitting or flying side by side and giving their deep, kind of self-satisfying cluck-cluck-cluck and see if it's not your sentiment exactly.*

*These paragraphs first appeared in Dan Abrams' Feb 26,1976 "Outdoors" column in the Jackson Hole News in Jackson, Wyoming. I wrote a guest shot on "The Uncommon Raven," of which the above is part. Still my sentiments.

❧ EUROPEAN STARLING ❧
Sturnus vulgaris

European starlings were "successfully" imported into North America just over a century ago, on the East Coast. Still capable of suprising natural history observers, this aggressive bird is still finding and reaching niches in the Northern Rockies and surrounding areas.

Writing about the starling only three decades after it was imported, Edward H. Forbush stated, "When any animal is successfully introduced into a new country, and increases rapidly, its advent tends to upset the biological balance." This immutable rule is apparent almost everywhere in the Rocky Mountain West, as its human population balloons with East and West Coast immigrants.

And it goes for starlings, too.

In the last quarter century this short-tailed, long-winged, chunky, flying triangle of a "blackbird" has become a familiar in the Northern Rockies. It, too, is affecting the fortunes of long-time residents, is taking over nesting holes from various other bird species, competes with true blackbirds and insect eaters, bullies everybody.

As winter wanes, the starling's bill turns a distinct yellow and its plumage becomes iridescent and flecked with greens, browns, and purples. Many an observer is disappointed, believing he has discovered something foreign or exotic, only to find out it is commonplace.

A familiar story.

꒰ HOUSE SPARROW ꒱
Passer domesticus

About the house sparrow, Richard Pough wrote, "The environment produced by the establishment of urban or agricultural civilization in any temperate area exactly suits the bird." To the extent that the Northern Rockies has been populated, if not civilized, one will find house sparrows in cities, towns, ranches or farms, and around businesses throughout.

The house sparrow was first introduced into North America in 1851. Many more importations followed, and it is now naturalized from Canada to South America. It is mostly absent from alpine, desert and densely forested regions, but that is by its own choice.

A clean house sparrow often surprises persons who have seen it only in cities where the birds cannot bathe adequately. It is a clear, light gray-breasted finch, sporting a black bib, a gray cheek patch, a gray crown and a chestnut nape. Pretty neat. Females and young birds lack the black throat, are a dull brown and perpetually dingy white below.

House sparrows, wherever found, are gregarious and also garrulous. Their various notes and "cheeeeps" can be – to put the kindest interpretation on it – unmusical, persistent and without much musical or other merit. To human ears. Obviously, not to each other.

AFTERWORDS ৵

There's an old geologist's saying to the effect that if he hadn't believed it, he would have never seen it. I actually knew that old geologist.

Finding birds in winter in the Northern Rockies is a little like searching for some previously unrecognized subtle or hidden geomorphic feature. They're there, but if you don't believe, you'll never see them.

Different from summer or spring.

What should your winter birding strategy be, then??

Just go out and look.

Many bird watchers think summer is the optimum time to find birds. True enough, there are more birds around. More species, more numbers of most species. True, but many birds are on the nest, quiet, and don't want to be seen, or are busy feeding and training their young and are no longer singing. Some are hiding out as only they can.

Summer birds are great. But winter birds, they're hardy souls with fewer obligations. Every wild creature has to be concerned about its safety and food. Winter birds have pretty much only those concerns—not territorial defenses, not mate selection, not eggs to brood, nor young to care for.

Why, winter birds are almost on vacation!

What better time to look for them?

INDEX ᔗ

BERT RAYNES

With his wife, Meg, Bert Raynes explored the United States as extensively as his workaholic career as a research chemical engineer allowed, avoiding cities and concentrating on remote areas, national parks and monuments. They soon found the Northern Rocky Mountain region the one they were most drawn to and in 1972 retired to Jackson Hole, Wyoming.

There they began a second life. Bert almost inadvertently became a nature writer, newspaper columnist and book author. His books include: *Birds of Grand Teton National Park, Valley So Sweet* and *Curmudgeon Chronicles.*

In 2000, Bert was awarded the Rungius Medal by the National Museum of Wildlife Art, joining a spectacular company that includes Mardy Murie, Wallace Stegner, Roger Tory Peterson, David J. Love and Jane Goodall. He still has difficulty in believing it.

THOMAS D. MANGELSEN

Devoted to a lifetime of documenting the natural world, Thomas D. Mangelsen is one of the world's premier nature photographers. Driven by expressing the beauty and intricacy of the wilderness, Tom spends up to nine months a year in the field. With his background in cinematography, his photographs tell a story of the habitat and surroundings of his subjects, evoking the world around the animal and the landscapes in which they make their home.

Tom received an Honorary Fellowship by The Royal Photographic Society in 2002, the North American Nature Photographer Association's (NANPA) Outstanding Nature Photographer of the Year 2000 award, and was chosen BBC's Wildlife Photographer of the Year in 1994. Tom's work has appeared in *Audubon, National Geographic, Life Magazine,* and *Wildlife Art.* His other books include *Images of Nature: the Photography of Thomas D. Mangelsen, Polar Dance: Born of the North Wind* and *Spirit of the Rockies: The Mountain Lions of Jackson Hole.* Tom lives in Moose, Wyoming, near the border of Grand Teton National Park.